DYING
TO LIVE

MICHAEL HOLLINGS

McCrimmons
Great Wakering Essex

First published 1991 by
McCrimmon Publishing Company Limited,
10–12 High Street, Great Wakering, Essex SS3 0EQ

© 1991 Michael Hollings

ISBN 0 85597 444 3

Cover by Nick Snode
Typesetting by Fleetlines, Southend
Typeset in Plantin, 11 on 12 point.
Printed by The Wolsey Press Ltd, Ipswich

Contents

Dying to Live | 1

With complete fearlessness I shall go on, so that, now as always, Christ will be glorified in my body, whether by my life or my death. Life to me, of course, is Christ, but then death would be a positive gain. (Phil 1:20–21)

I visit a home for the elderly. I stop with an eighty year old, ex-civil servant – Melissa. She is bright as a button, almost blind, very happy and chatty. I tell her I'm not going to give her a kiss, because I have 'flu. She at once replies 'Oh! Give me a kiss! You might give me some germs – and I do want to die, but I just seem to go on'.

I visit a hospital where Priscilla in her mid-eighties has broken her hip. She is in a lot of pain – but bright, the nurses are wonderful, she'll soon be out she's told – then she can live again – there's lots of life in me still, she says.

A woman comes in to see me carrying a small child in her arms, with two other kids trailing behind her. Tears! Her husband is only thirty. He has been given three weeks to live – terminal cancer. How can God do that to me? – Look at my children! How can I cope! I hate God! He's not fair to kill Tommy. God can't be good!

Each of us is different. Each of us reacts differently to the immediate shock, horror, despair and grief of terminal illness and death.

Yet we do have something in common – each of us will die. We cannot escape that truth, hide it though we may. Day or time is not revealed to us.

The Catholic teaching has for a long time been a suggestion that we think of death and the after life not now and then, but daily when we go to bed. I'm afraid we are not very good at facing the truth; not for others – but for us – for me!

Each of us is both living to die – and also probably dying to live! The object of these few pages is to help us do both these things in practical ways. If we can face these inevitable sorrows and challenges in a sober, matter of fact way, peacefully and even with joy, we shall be strengthened ourselves and be of much more practical help to others around us.

A note for priests and hospital chaplains

You will have had a wide range of experience in sickness, terminal illness, dying and death, funeral arrangements and bereavement. I do not imagine there is anything new to you in what I have put down here.

I hope there is nothing outrageous in these pages, but there may be omissions or things which should be omitted, or things which could be put better. If so, please let us know so that it can be changed at a later time.

> *Lord, in good health I want to praise and thank you – and I often forget. In sickness, I want to get better and pray for your healing power. Sometimes, I blame you. Please help me to live in hope, while looking calmly and deeply at life and death. You are Lord of life. I thank you for the life you have given me. Strengthen my life, my love and my trust. Amen.*

Facing the truth | 2

I am the Way; I am Truth and Life. (Jn 14:6). I came into the world for this, to bear witness to the truth; and all who are on the side of truth listen to my voice. 'Truth' said Pilate, 'What is that?' (Jn 18:37)

There is a passage in the Acts of the Apostles telling how Peter is faced by an unpalatable truth. A pagan, Cornelius, and his household have mysteriously received the Holy Spirit. The family are not Jews, they are not of the chosen people, so Peter is given a vision of all kinds of animals, including those excluded by the law, and told to take them and eat.

Through his vision Peter comes to declare 'I now really understand that God has no favourites, but that anybody of any nationality who fears him and does what is right is acceptable to him' (Acts 10:34–35).

Truth is often awkward. We do not want to face the truth for one reason or another. Recently I was giving a talk at a meeting of Catholic social workers. During the day the Chaplain celebrated Mass. He introduced the celebration by welcoming me. He added that when I came in to give my talk, one of the audience turned to him and said: 'Now we can see how we are all ageing'! An unpalatable truth, but it has to be admitted, lived with and enjoyed.

What is it about us that we find it very hard to face the truth, even in quite small things? If you are at all like me, you will probably find yourself concealing the truth, telling 'half-truths' and so on.

To be truthful is to be humble. Jesus, who is the Way, the Truth and the Life, told us only once to learn of him. He said 'Learn of me, because I am meek and humble of heart' (Matthew 11:29).

My key to the awkwardness of facing the truth is humility. Essentially I am an individual – a very private person: I want my space, my freedom, my own privacy. And so it is an invasion of ME at any time that I am asked a question. It is even more an invasion when I have to strip off and be examined in and out by a doctor who probes and asks most intimate questions. He or she does it most professionally, but it still invades me and even more so when I am put into hospital and my freedom curtailed.

That reaction is pretty silly of me really, isn't it? What is being done is for me, my health, my well being – and I resent it! The way forward is to be open and humble and face the truth that I am human, I am imperfect; I need others' help and so I must not pretend I don't.

Of course, part of the reason is fear. I am normally genuinely scared of what the doctor may say. It may be as simple as 'lose weight', or as questionable as 'I am going to send you for an

X-ray'. Whichever or whatever, I am inclined to think the worst – turn a cough into bronchitis, an ache into arthritis, a shortage of breath into heart trouble – and so on.

Personally, I had a very good experience which has helped me laugh at myself and my fears. In World War II, I was in a battle – standing with a friend, a fellow officer, on a mountainside in Italy, in snow, ice and bitter cold. We were both wrapped up with coats, scarves, mufflers etc. Violent shelling began very close to us, and we both fell to the ground as mortar bombs exploded nearby. I felt a sudden agonising pain from the back of my neck. I said nothing to my companion till we were back in our dugout. Then I said, feeling very brave 'Bob, could you have a look – I think I've been wounded in the back of my neck'. I took off my scarf and Bob burst into laughter. I asked what was so funny? He said I had not been wounded – I had a huge carbuncle on the back of my neck! It took me a long time to live that down, but it taught me a lesson – always hope for the best, rather than expect the worst.

Fear is very real. I do not believe that there is any one of us human beings who is literally without fear. Some may say they are never afraid, but then they may not have been through the particular situation which will trigger fear in them.

If life deteriorates in quality, if it falters and fails, it becomes more immediately necessary to think of death, judgement and life-after-death. Then, should not every person have access to the truth of their condition?

From my background and way of life, first as a Catholic layman and since then as a priest, I cannot accept that it is generally right for anyone to go forward to an unprepared death. As I grew up, the 'last sacraments' – the anointing of a sick person – were regarded as a death warrant. Many families did not call a priest in until the sick person was unconscious, for fear the person might be frightened.

Once, twenty years ago, I was in an old people's home visiting and giving Holy Communion. I noticed an elderly man at the end of the ward who was in floods of tears.

I decided I would go and talk to him at the end of my round. As I approached him, he looked up and shouted out 'B..... off you! I'm not dying yet'. Happily anointing has become much more acceptable without the implication of immediate death.

This sacrament can be a very good 'way in' approach to any illness, terminal or not. It is particularly effective if there can be 'healing services' with anointing of the sick as the regular celebration in any parish. Apart from being a wonderful spiritual community experience, healing of its very self in many different ways, it brings illness into a public forum. We are all of us imperfect and it is clear from daily occurences that a 'perfectly fit' one of us may die suddenly of a heart attack, be diagnosed as having cancer, have a stroke. Young, old and middling – each of us is subject to illness and death, from cot death to fading away in the eighties or nineties.

Particularly as a pastoral work for priests, it is important to be able to talk and listen to anyone who is sick. If lips are sealed, if relations are in disarray, the priest has a dilemma – how much does he know – what can he share? Where must he be silent? As a priest I can say that it is possible to be totally at sea in a particular situation. Every individual and family is different. But I believe it is important in visiting, listening, being about, that there should also be inculcated through preaching and other means a general attitude towards sickness, dying and death, which will encourage hope and peace, rather than fear.

Patient, doctor, nurse, relation, priest, friend – think about secrecy and silence – discuss it among yourselves. You may not agree with what I write and what I practise myself – but at least face the issue and thoughtfully, prayerfully develop a policy. This should not be rigid, but informed with the love of God in Jesus Christ – and the love of self, of brother and sister – seeking a sensitive way to be dying to live.

> *You, Lord, are the truth. Give me/us courage to face the truth. It is often easier to hide from unwelcome facts, to pretend there is nothing wrong. Help us to be honest with ourselves and others. Give us the sensitivity not to hurt or be hurt, but to accept humbly our share of your way of the cross and your life devoted to doing the will of your Father in love through you, Jesus, Son of God.*

Silence and secrecy | 3

You cannot love too much, only in the wrong way. (Traherne). Nothing is hidden but it will be made clear, nothing secret but it will be made known and brought to light. So take care how you listen. (Lk 8:17–18)

Silence and secrecy have an effect well beyond an individual. In more recent times, some speakers and writers have used the phrase 'conspiracy of silence'. This often refers to the silence of surgeons, doctors etc. The silence refers to a disinclination on the part of the doctor to talk about 'terminal illness', to give a prognosis which includes death.

The work of the medical profession is to heal, to give relief from suffering, to reassure. The individual person's fear of facing the truth, the unwillingness to put themselves in the power of another person, conspires with the hidden reluctance of the medically trained person to face his or her own impotence in the seemingly inevitable advance of a 'lethal' disease. It is part of an upbringing, of a philosophy, of a whole way of life, to support the patient with care and sensitivity. How right that is,

15

and surely that is exactly what a patient would expect from a doctor.

Unhappily, the expectation of the patient and the professional attitude of the doctor may in practice work together towards secrecy. I'm sure physicians and surgeons of all lands have thought very deeply about this question. I am not suggesting an absolute or insensitive revelation of truth. But the general christian outlook should be that it is better to know the truth than to hide it. It is also true that the human being is tougher and less fragile than is sometimes indicated.

Now, there is a real possibility that the silence and secrecy extends its blanket to the family and friends of the individual who is under the doctor. It may not seem very important at the beginning of an illness. Everything may well be in the air – no final diagnosis, etc. There can then be built up a false support system based on an unsupported hope that all is well. An almost-game emerges with all the parties concerned pretending like mad how well the patient is as things get worse.

I give you an instance of this. A young man of eighteen or nineteen, very much in love with a beautiful girl of the same age, developed cancer of the genitals. He had to go through chemotherapy. He was not told he had cancer. I spoke to the physician who said his parents refused to let him or his girl know the score. I begged his parents to allow him to know. That the young couple might well want to marry immediately if they knew. Total refusal. About a month before his death, the young man and his girl came to realise the truth. He died without being able to marry. The illness had taken more than a year, during which, full of hope, they had continually put off marrying till he was well again.

It can be argued that it is better all round if the sick person does not know what is wrong, or his or her condition. I well remember hearing on the radio of the death of a well known actor or media personality. One of his friends said over the air 'Thank God, he did not know he was dying'.

I do not know whether he or his friend were Christians. What would your reaction be to this attitude of secrecy? How do you – how would you – react to this situation in your own life, among your family and friends? Practically, this question should be answered by each of us from our different angles.

The answer should centre on the meaning and purpose of our individual daily living, the purpose of life. Created by God, I am to live in his world as fully as I can. He has given me a mind to think with, a freedom of will. If I have been fortunate enough to be given faith in God and his purpose, then I know that I am only here temporarily to make the most of all I am, to love him and my neighbour and so on – all this leading to eternal life. I should – I may not – live this commitment!

But just as it is essential for us to face the truth, so it is essential that we face fear. It gets us nowhere to pretend fear is not there. It is. If you, as it were, talk it out and look at it calmly: if you pray about it: if you are humble enough to share it with someone else, then I am sure you will find that it takes on quite a different colour and texture. This does not mean that it is far more easy to bear. But it can now be looked at coolly, assessed rationally and lived with from day to day.

A new fear and personal need for secrecy has emerged with the discovery of AIDS. Because all publicity focuses on the relation between AIDS and homosexual activity or 'shooting-up' with drugs, those who are diagnosed as HIV positive and full AIDS invasion of their system often feel extremely shy of revealing their condition. This is very understandable owing to bad publicity, and also a strong, though often 'gut' reaction which is not thought out sufficiently. Given the social climate, it is often extremely difficult for an individual to admit their sexuality, if it is inclined to the same sex. But sexuality is a private matter. No one needs, unless they want to, to go round saying: 'I'm heterosexual, I'm homosexual.'

However, if a person feels strong enough, it can be a great help to be open, though I realize from what I have heard from others, that honesty and openness is not always the best policy. Nevertheless, having been with, worked with and come to know and love a considerable number of HIV and positively AIDS infected people, I just want to say that I have learned a great deal from them. Each person (once again I say it!) is different. But I have found so much of positive growth and development among those who have faced up to their affliction that I would want any who feel they can to gently tell those who are near and those who care. A number of very holy people are being reborn through the scourge of AIDS. If you can bear it, whoever you are suffering from AIDS, try to share your knowledge discreetly, gain support, prayers, understanding and love. You will need this support and so will your friends and relations. If you survive your ordeal, if you come through and live, how much you will have to give. If you die, how much of an apostle you will have been – in any event, praise the Lord for he is good!

We love and cherish our privacy, Lord. We are often secret people. Well, Lord, you are a hidden God, but you have chosen to reveal yourself to those you love so much we would not have known through Jesus and the Holy Spirit. Assist us to get right the balance between silent secrecy and openness.

The value of sharing | 4

Come to me, all you who labour and are overburdened, and I will give you rest. Shoulder my yoke and learn from me, for I am gentle and humble in heart and you will find rest for your souls. Yes, my yoke is easy and my burden light. (Matthew 11:28–30)

In a beautiful section of the Book of Ecclesiastes, the author writes:

There is a season for everything, a time for every occupation under heaven:

> A time for giving birth
> A time for dying...
> A time for healing
> A time for tears,
> A time for laughter,
> A time for mourning
> A time for dancing...
> A time for embracing...
> A time for keeping silent,
> A time for searching...
> A time for losing...

A time for keeping...
A time for giving away...
A time for speaking
A time for loving
A time for peace.

Eccles. 3:1–8

In the last chapter, we have looked a little at silence and secrecy and I have urged a greater openness. I think it is clear that in the very varied life which God has created, we do differ from each other a great deal – but also have much in common. It is the changing kaleidoscope of our times which makes it difficult and inappropriate to lay down too many broad, sweeping rules of conduct. There are so many different persons, times and seasons, the combination calls for openness and sensitivity, for gentle development and for sharing.

Although the poet tells us 'no man is an island', there is the freedom of individuality which makes it possible for anyone to isolate himself or herself. Indeed, some writer once put it that 'loneliness is the price of individuality'.

So, it is not simply a desire which isolates, but also inevitably – and particularly in death itself, that each one of us is alone. This is true when bereavement occurs, when a personal decision has to be made – or when one is lying in pain by day or night. However, there is real danger that the loneliness and isolation can be increased rather than broken down by silence, by secrecy, by shyness, by inability to share.

One of the main strands of christianity is the emphasis on each of us trying to love one another. Now we cannot do this if we don't know each other and if we are not prepared to share with each other.

I suppose it is asking a lot for a person to become more open at a time of crisis, when that openness has not been practised in daily living over the years.

Trusting another person is difficult. In a perfect world, we might be able to trust everyone. As we live today, only too many people know how they can be exploited – taken to the cleaners – by trusting the wrong person. Again and again, especially with the elderly, I have to warn against opening the door to strangers, confiding personal circumstances to strangers, and so on. A great deal of pain and suffering comes through simple-hearted sharing with another but unknown person. Beware of that, please. But what I am writing about now is rather different.

The positive side of openness and sharing is that whole new depths of relationship open up. It is astonishing how much we do conceal from each other, perhaps more especially when very ugly or serious matters are concerned. An illustration which has nothing to do with sickness or death and is not told as a proselytising story is this. A Baptist minister came to talk to me. He said he wanted to become a Roman Catholic, but not until he retired in a few years time. He said his wife was a strong Anglican and she did not know his desire. I suggested he kept in touch with me and at some time talked to his wife. I met his wife and he visited me frequently until, a couple of years later he came,

23

announced he had retired and asked what next. I said we could begin instruction when he liked – but, if he had not done so already, he should tell his wife. 'Oh dear,' he said, 'she'll be very upset!' However, he went off to tell her. After two days he came back, saying he was shattered! Very tentatively he had said to his wife: 'My dear, I'm afraid you will be very upset. I've got to tell you that I've decided to become a Roman Catholic.' She immediately replied, 'I'm so glad, I have wanted to be a Roman Catholic for years!'

This very close and loving and spiritual couple had never shared that 'shared' desire. When they did, it was a breakthrough which further deepened their love.

My experience has been that many relationships involving sickness and terminal illness which have been shared have grown in love and caring, with many areas coming to light which had previously been hidden.

A friend of mine introduced me to a couple. In the first place, I did what I could to help with their son who was unreliable and took drugs. Very sadly he eventually died of an overdose, but in its pain-shared way, this tragedy drew them closer. It seemed to pave the way for an event which came upon them suddenly very soon after his death – his mother was diagnosed as having advanced cancer of the pancreas. Now there began a time when her husband, who had previously had great difficulty with money and with drink, turned to looking after her completely. From a very formalized religious practice, they came to share Eucharist at the bedside, prayer together, nearness of the family. When she found it increasingly hard to pray, I suggested the rosary, and it became a great source of laughter as her husband was repeatedly complaining he had to spend his time searching for the rosary beads among her bed clothes. When she became too weak to concentrate, he played tapes of the rosary softly to her. Sitting with them one afternoon in her bedroom at home, they said together: 'You know, we have never been happier.'

There was a great sense of peace and joy as she faded away. When she died, they had certainly never been closer or more deeply in love.

It would be stupid of me to give the impression that sharing is the answer to a sad, hard situation which involves suffering, anger, remorse and almost every emotion. No! It is because the situation is so human and so painful that sharing is so much more real and positive than a growing awareness of the true situation which is not discussed or shared – hidden as a silent secret to be kept private.

There is a wider sharing which is valuable. It extends between doctor and patient, doctor and the family, a close neighbour or a long standing friend. It can (and I think should) include the priest.

Whereas, at its worst, sickness seems something to hide and be ashamed of, sharing provides a support which is a wonderful resource.

THE VALUE OF SHARING

If we are human, we have to realise and not be worried about the effect it has on our emotions, both as sufferer, and friend or relation. We simply are not normally people who accept unquestioningly what is happening. There is shock to be absorbed, resentment against doctors, the world, nearest and dearest and perhaps especially God. In this situation it is good that there is someone or more than one with whom it is possible to be completely free, to let out fear and doubt, anger and resentment, and emptiness and ennui – the desire to end it all, a sense of personal failure and a strange self guilt which seeks relief by a desire to attack as well as to wallow in misery.

We are indeed complicated people! In this particular situation, I personally find one of the wonders of my life in the priesthood. If we accept that God is the one who listens, then his priest should be a listener. Very often there is not much else which is possible or necessary. Listening can be a real sharing. The listener can be like a sponge which absorbs the worries, hates, tears, bitterness and so on of the one who is sharing. Doctors, nurses, counsellors, family and friends should in different ways all be available for listening and supporting. But we have to face the fact that, as different individuals, our capacity for listening and sharing varies. Priests and professionals can both be taught skills in listening, and also can learn from prayer and experience how to be a sponge. Each other person, to his or her capacity, can grow in skill, sensitivity, patience and openness.

THE VALUE OF SHARING

God of love, you share your life with us because you love us so much. Teach us to share our lives more and more deeply with you, to help us to share more with each other. For some of us, it is so difficult to share things which are intimate to us. Open our minds and hearts that we may be generous with ourselves and our time. Make us good listeners, people of warmth, support and peace, through Christ the Prince of Peace.

Terminal care | 5

'Lord, the man you love is ill'. On receiving
the message, Jesus said, 'This sickness will
not end in death, but is for God's glory so
that through it the Son of God may be
glorified.' (Jn 11:3–4)

This title is rather chilling and perhaps it is
necessary to talk round it.

The first hospice as I know of them existed in
London. It was St Joseph's Hospice for the Dying,
Mare Street, Hackney. At some point of time which
I forget, the title was discreetly changed to St
Joseph's Hospice. Since then there has grown up
the whole developing Hospice movement and the
care of those who probably have only a limited time
to live. This has been a wonderful acceptance of the
challenge to help any and everyone to have as full a
life as possible, so that they are enabled to live with
their personal dignity.

As you may imagine, in the course of my life I
have shared in and witnessed a great number of
illnesses which ended in death.

For me one of the most personal and poignant
was the dying of my mother. I was in Italy during

World War II. She wrote that she had an incurable cancer – could I come home? Owing to large casualties we were having an amalgamation of two battalions at that time. I was among those due to go home – until my opposite number who was due to stay took me on one side. He told me he was in his forties (I was about twenty-two) and that he had a wife and four children in England. Could he go home instead of me? I had to say 'yes' to that. Then a few months later, when the war in Europe ended, I got home to find my mother thin, tired, in pain but full of joy that I was home. She knew she was incurable, but went on fighting. We had a horrific time, as we had no home and she stayed for a time in a hotel, while I was on leave.

Then my sister and I got her to a happy, friendly nursing home with immense personal care. But I was still in the army and could only come occasionally over a few weeks to sit with her, to be silent, to care for her when she was in pain or vomiting. Then the army posted me to Palestine. I had the sorrow of leaving her dying – I was summoned by cable from Palestine, but was not allowed home. She died without my seeing her again.

Difficult as it was for me, this close encounter with death, which was backed by much violent death in my war years, gave me a foundation which I did not seek or want or enjoy. But from these individuals and these circumstances I learned a great deal, largely through blundering and mistakes. These did not make me skilled, but opened up for me the chaos of emptiness and powerlessness when meeting all degrees of sickness, all kinds of dying, all anxieties, different individuals' fears and worries.

Such is the variety and time span of illness that it often confounds professional doctors, nurses and counsellors. How can they say what they do not know? It is possible, given particular circumstances and a particular disease, that some prognosis may be hazarded. But I have learned over the years the serious concern that doctors and other professionals have. If they give a short life outlook, the patient may rally and live on indefinitely; or they may give a long life hope – and the patient dies almost immediately! But attitudes are so important. It is certainly possible to be sensitive to the 'demands' of patient and relations, or to be brusque and defensive. It is the latter which makes both patient and relatives feel brushed off, unimportant or ignored. They feel shut out from sharing a desperately important personal and intimate human relationship by the professional who to them is an outsider. But he or she, doctor or nurse, is also an insider because they normally have more knowledge and skill than any of those seeking information.

If you are coming to a hospital to visit a sick relative, it may often seem that everyone is so busy that it is impossible to pin anyone down to give you what you consider vital information. It is true that they are mostly very busy and at the present time very understaffed. It is for those of us who are not professionally engaged to realize and accept the pressure upon doctors and nurses and general staff.

Nevertheless, we can justifiably ask and if we wait in patience, we will eventually receive the information we seek, at least in part.

Sit down a moment, whoever you are, from whatever angle you come – and think what you are wanting to do, what is your hope, your expectation? I ask this because my sense is that the sick person is the central pre-occupation of any and every person. If that is not so, it should be. We are not involved to prove something, to gain something for ourselves, we are there for the one who is sick. In the midst of this, one of the hardest moments which comes is when we realize it may well be better for that sick person, this patient, this one we love so deeply – perhaps should die. The future is in the next world, and not in being rehabilitated into the present world.

This is not an easy decision to come to in oneself. Turning off the life support system is the ultimate decision, which thankfully may never happen. Before that it is a personal work coming to terms with the suffering and the desire to heal and to alleviate pain.

Great strides have been taken in the control of pain in recent years. The growth of the Hospice Movement has been of immense benefit to very many who have been fortunate enough to be enfolded in the loving care of a hospice staff. This is not written to set on one side the ordinary hospital care or the work of the local GP. Both are indispensable. But I have much fellow feeling for both hospital and GP, because the priest in a parish has considerable similarity with them. I know what it is to be a Jack of all trades. This is what a priest in a parish is about – because he is involved in birth, marriage and death. He is there in sickness or in health – in joy or sorrow – in the ordinary day by day slog of minor ups and downs, the coughs and colds of the medical world. In the same way, a hospital is a many-sided organization from emergency and casualty to geriatric care. Though it is possible to have wards organized for various needs – maternity, children, geriatric, medical, surgical, etc – especially with the present state of the Health Service, resources are spread thin. This can mean that there is not as much time as ideally doctor or nurse or patient would require. This sets up a tension and a sense of busy-ness which detracts from the atmosphere of patient-care.

I have visited numerous hospitals over the years, and been hospitalized myself. There have been many different experiences, seen from different angles – personal, nurses, doctors, ward orderlies, patients and their relatives. Where there have been wards for the elderly and the terminal, there has been a greater possibility of a more relaxed and personal approach for all the staff. Just recently I have been for a long period visiting a very disting-uished elderly man who sadly had Alzheimer's disease. But his wife who visited him for weeks and months could not give sufficient praise to the staff of the ward for their warmth, care and attention, not only to the patients, but to the visitors whom they cherished equally. Indeed, when my old friend died – peacefully serene and surrounded by love –

the ward sister even came to his requiem.

The Hospice Movement has the great advantage that the individual hospices are specialized – their purpose and function is centred on the terminally ill. Far from this bringing a gloomy, morbid atmosphere, the smallness and the specialist approach makes for greater flexibility. I find when I go to visit individuals in a hospice that there is a sense of light and joy, of warmth and hope.

It is often possible through this system for a person to come to spend time in the hospice and then to go home for a period, being re-admitted when necessary. This gives a flexibility which helps to remove fear, lends a sense of freedom in coming and going, and eases the return when this becomes inevitable.

An extension of this service in some places makes it possible for those who are in the care of the hospice to have home visits to support the family of the sick person. This kind of regular input is of considerable importance for the patient. To be at home is a primary desire for so many. But the sad fact is that the joy of being at home is offset by the difficulty a husband or wife or family meet in priority care up to the standard of a hospital or hospice. In some ways the personal love and devotion from close family is unmatchable in hospital or hospice. But there is not 'off-duty', the facilities are not available, there will be strain and irritation. Family, patient, doctor and nurse have to weigh the pros and cons. It can be wonderful when the centrality of home outweighs everything else, but it is therefore very hard on all concerned when it is clearly right that it really is better for everyone that the patient should be re-admitted to hospital or hospice. People feel guilty, inadequate, let down – so many things. However, the sick person is central to what is happening. All our personal hurts must be put aside in order to ease the sick person forward in what to him or her is a viable way of life.

I have been part of many different methods and treatments in the terminal months and weeks of individual lives. To me there is no doubt that for a considerable number of people, home is the priority beyond all else. We might then ask – how is this possible? Well, it varies a great deal because of the circumstances. Quite a number of elderly and single persons cling on to their little piece of ownership and privacy. Being at home helps to retain their human dignity. No child, who could think at all, would want to be 'in care'. So no older person really wants to be 'in care'. Independence – even when waited on hand and foot – means a great deal. 'Independence' is often tied to 'a place of my own, my own front door' etc.

Voluntary work among the parishioners *can* help with this when SVP, pastoral committees or other individual parishioners are prepared to come in and help out the statutory services. But it can be much easier when there is family about, and the family rallying round is a great way of getting together and making the last period one of love and care in a home atmosphere. But this is not an easy undertaking as should be understood. Care becomes more and more full time and very, very heavy for one person. It may just not be possible. When it is, an immense benefit warms all concerned.

I think two of the happiest deaths I have shared in different places were when the dying persons – both grandmothers – were in bed in the main living room of the home, surrounded by sons and daughers, grandsons and grand-daughters, with the family life continuing, the TV on, meals taking place, general conversation. This continued for the last weeks and right through to death. I felt if it had been me, I would have been driven mad by the TV, the comings and goings, the noise and bustle of all ages of life. However, in both cases, the ladies were peaceful and happy, joined in, slept, lost consciousness, came back into the pulse of life – and eventually had most of the family and myself around the bed as they went to God. Such a scenario would not be ideal or even appropriate for many – but it brings one to think that dying alone can be a terribly sad way to leave this world. Each of us is essentially alone in death – but to me bedside support has grown to seem more appropriate and to be attempted if at all possible.

However, such a statement by me should not make anyone feel guilty if the demand is too great. Should home be overtired and stressed, this will certainly not help the patient. Commonsense and the humility to accept the need of rest must come into the equation. Even when the dying person is in hospital, the strain on next of kin can be too much. Hospitals often try to ease the burden by allowing a close relative to stay overnight. This is not always possible. I have found that the nursing staff generally keep an eye on relatives who spend long hours in a ward or at a bedside. And so they will sometimes urge people to go home at night and have a good rest and sleep. This can worry the tired-out relatives who feel duty-bound to stay, in case death should occur. But it is best to take the hospital's advice. Occasionally a sudden change will take place, but you will be called back immediately, and please God you will get there in time.

Finally, if we have been praying, we must come to see that death, though not our immediate desire, may be an answer to our prayer.

The dying

When people are near to death or even some way before, different moods can seize them. For those alongside them or visiting them, it is useful to be aware that this is so, so that there can be tolerance and sensitivity. It can be awkward if a lot of anger is vented on the nearest and dearest. This is natural and perhaps to be expected, but it can really upset a devoted wife or husband to be apparently accused of this or that. There may be intense depression bordering on despair, or a tired lethargy which does not respond to anything, even though the patient is fully conscious. Fretfulness and continuous demands become tiring and irritating, and call for patience.

Some people lose consciousness and remain unconscious over a prolonged period. Conscious or unconscious, the use of touch is very important – more especially so in unconsciousness. Often to be sitting by someone, simply gently holding a hand or touching an arm is a source of real comfort and support, when other communication is tiring. The warmth of a kiss penetrates and soothes.

No one is altogether clear how much an unconscious person hears or understands. But some interesting tests have been done to try to assess reaction, especially with patients who have suffered severe injuries from accidents. My practice is to talk gently but clearly and simply to an unconscious person, as well as holding a hand and kissing them on arrival and departure. I try to repeat short reassuring phrases and often say aloud an Our Father, a Hail Mary or a decade of the Rosary. And, of course, I tell them who I am!

With this in mind, it is wise to be careful of loud discussion among friends or relatives about the dying person within their possible hearing. I am sure that it is never a waste of time to sit with an unconscious person, provided there is hand contact and the occasional vocal effort.

Lord God, you make us and you know what we are like. We are afraid of dying and death. And so the acceptance of a terminal illness is very hard for the sufferer and the relations and friends alike. We so much need your compassion and care to touch us. We need your strength and your love, so that we can go forward together into the unknown confident that you are always with us, and that you accept the depth of our uncertainty and will help us to support each other in patience and love. Thank you, Lord.

Practical matters | 6

*'Go and make preparations for us to eat the
Passover.' (Lk 22:15)*

'Have you made your will?' I asked an elderly lady,
living by herself. 'Oh no', she replied. 'I've got
nothing to leave anyone, so I haven't bothered.'

Have you made your will?

Perhaps the question is wrong. But my other
possible question sounds much more bold – 'Have
you made arrangements for your death and
funeral?'

I suppose it is difficult enough to face up to the
truth of our mortality without planning for death!
But there are very real and positive reasons for me
to suggest what follows.

Firstly, let me say that though I have nothing
much to leave, I have made my will! My reason for
this is firstly that the Diocese lays down that every
priest must make a will. Right – done! But my own
personal concern is that I should not be a nuisance
when I die. I see it as important that those left to
care for my mortal remains should have as clear and
easy a job as possible. So I have given details of my

next of kin. I have left directions in a simple way for my funeral, including cremation and where, in a corner of an existing grave, my ashes may be placed.

I am making a point of this because it can seem a chore and a waste of time to make such arrangements. As a priest I have found over and over again that there is chaos, wasted time, heartbreak and tears because a person dies, no one knows the next of kin, everyone searches, the dead body cannot be given a decent funeral. Sometimes weeks upon weeks have gone by and eventually there is no full Catholic funeral, because the local council simply takes over and does a 'pauper's' funeral straight to the cemetery.

Early arrangements can be sorted out privately by individuals. What we try to do where I live and work is to make ourselves available for anyone who would like to make some provision for their death. If there is a will to be made, we have two or three solicitors prepared to help. (I'm sure almost every parish could find volunteer help in this way.) But otherwise we simply get a note from the person concerned which will include next of kin, executor if there is one, arrangements desired for the funeral – Mass, burial or cremation and so on. Some individuals like to think out the form of the Mass, Latin or English or native tongue, the readings, hymns and so on.

If anyone should say that he or she has not reached that stage yet, let me tell you that we have been holding a number of these wills for long periods. To make sensible provision for death is certainly not a death sentence! Indeed it can be said that the settling of some of these details gives a security and sense of relief – takes away some of the tensions and worries which are injurious to health.

Before dying and death: *I don't really want to think about arrangements for my death, Lord. But I do not want to be a nuisance. So would you help me, Lord, to be sensible and practical, to make my will and to see how I can arrange everything in such a way that it may be simple and unembarrass-ing for my family and friends. Give me a peace of mind which clears my muddle and my fear. I do want to save those I love and to leave behind me a warm feeling of care for them, while they can do a service for me.*

After death. *O God, O God, O God! He/She is dead. Though I knew it would happen, I can't believe it. Oh my tears and my sorrow. But, Lord, help me to do all I should, so that my loved one can have a lovely, peaceful farewell for all of us. Give me the support to deal with all the little details and to be serene and even joyful… then I can give comfort to others who need it as much as I. And may he/she rest in peace with you as I now pray with all my trust and all the love of my heart. Amen.*

Immediately after death |

> *On arriving, Jesus found that Lazarus had been in the tomb for four days already... Many Jews had come to Martha and Mary to comfort them about their brother. When Martha heard Jesus was coming she went to meet him. Mary remained sitting in the house. Martha said to Jesus, 'Lord, if you had been here, my brother would not have died.'... Jesus said to her, 'Your brother will rise again.' (Jn 11:17–23)*

However death has occurred, any relation or friend will receive a severe shock. We may have been watching the slow fading away over weeks or months, knowing death is near at hand, sometimes almost willing it to happen. Yet the actual happening is still stunning. Or it may have been a sudden death: a heart attack at home or in the street, a wife waking to find her husband has died beside her in his sleep, or vice versa – shattering. Only too often today there is the short, sharp horror of an accident – on the road, at work, a disaster striking a theatre, a gas blow-out in a tower block, a cot death, a suicide.

Whatever way we are hit, there are things to be done. Activity in itself is therapeutic, because the emptiness of death drives us to want to do something.

Clearly, I want to say that the Catholic, the Christian, will want to involve the Church in the anxiety, fear, joy, sense of relief, guilt, desire that the dying/dead person is given all possible aid through the ministry of the Church. Though the anointing may have been done before, it is a real peace and joy for the dying person, as well as for relations and friends, if the ceremony and sacrament is done again, however close to death the patient is.

The person who has died needs our prayers. More immediately, those bereaved need sympathy, our presence, the physical contact of touch, embrace, literally a shoulder to weep on. Words are often totally ineffective or even useless.

BUT IT IS IMPORTANT TO BE THERE!

One of the awful parts of bereavement is that some people overwhelm you with too much sympathy, advice and encouragement. But many avoid you like the plague. The former mean so well, but the priority need at this stage is presence together with warmth and listening capability. Almost all exhortations can be empty or even false. In some ways the desire to say something meaningful comes from our own insecurity, our desire to say the right thing. Without realising it, we are concerned with ourselves and our appearance. The same is true from the other end – we stay away because we are shy, don't know what to say or are afraid of butting in. But why these doubts and fears? Is our concern for the bereaved person, or for me and you – guarding our pride, afraid of the difficulty of communication with a bereaved person.?

Practical things to do:

1. Get the Doctor:

a. If death is in hospital, this will have been done for you.

b. If death is at home, you must call the doctor as soon as possible to certify death. He will come as quickly as he can. Normally he will certify the death and write the medical certificate. This is in a sealed envelope addressed to the registrar, with a formal notice stating he has signed the certificate.

c. If the person has died suddenly, it may be necessary to have a post mortem to ascertain the cause of death. There is nothing wrong with this. Do not be worried. It is a legal requirement and it is a safeguard. This may mean a day or two of waiting. The coroner looks after it all and contacts the undertaker when it is complete, and the registrar is issued with a pink certificate and registers the death.

2. Get the Priest:

All possible spiritual help can be expected though the last sacraments should have been completed. But in the event of sudden death, the priest can come to pray and anoint. In any case it can be very comforting to have prayers round the body of the dead person, before the undertaker comes.

3. The Undertaker or Funeral Director

Once there is a death certificate from the doctor, or a decision on a post mortem, the undertaker can come to take the dead person's body to the funeral parlour or to the coroner's building.

The profession of undertaker requires a mixture of calmness, sympathy, efficiency, flexibility and patience. This is to extend to the secretary/telephonist who may frequently be a go-between and has a considerable influence both over the telephone and also in the office itself.

When we call or visit the undertaker, we are normally in shock and grief, often undecided what we want and surrounded by things that have to be arranged.

Be at peace and expect great care and attention and flexibility, where you will find every effort made to put you at ease and work out with you all the ins and outs of what you need to do and what you want to plan.

Of course, if some planning has been done beforehand – as I have already suggested – this makes the situation much simpler.

Lord God, you know all things. You know how distressed I am. Please give me strength to cope with all the details and arrangements which face me. Please give me support from family and friends... but not too much, Lord. I feel very fragile, but I want so much to do all I can to make the plans and to be open to those who come to grieve. Lord, help the undertaker and those who have to play a part in saying goodbye to the one I love. I trust you, Lord, and I rely upon your Spirit of love and compassion to be with me. Through Jesus your Son, Amen.

Before and during the funeral | 8

Joseph went to Pilate and asked for the body of Jesus. He then took it and wrapped it in a shroud and put it in a tomb which was hewn in stone and had never held a body...

Meanwhile the women who had come from Galilee with Jesus were following behind. They took note of the tomb and how the body had been laid. Then they returned and prepared spices and ointments.

On the first day of the week, at the first sign of dawn, they went to the tomb, with the spices they had prepared. (Lk.23.52–56; 24.1)

People from differing backgrounds give different expression to grief and have a different approach to the time gap between death and the funeral.

Irish people during my early priesthood used very normally to have the body of the deceased person brought home. The coffin was then opened and a 'wake' took place – frequently lasting throughout the night. This custom, which may have originated with missionary priests, is strongly carried on by families from the Caribbean. Prayers take place at home on the evening of the day of death. Very often, this is a prayer/song and social occasion each evening until the funeral, with many relatives, friends and neighbours coming from far and wide, and much prayer and many hymns sung. The family appreciate the visit of a priest and often like a mass to be said in the room where the person died. Sometimes his or her body is brought back to spend a day and night in the home.

If the deceased person's body is moved to the undertaker's funeral parlour, then anyone can visit and pray in a chapel of rest, where the coffin lies open, with the times arranged mutually. Some families appreciate being at the funeral parlour when the coffin is closed. At a West Indian funeral, the family may ask that the coffin be opened during the Mass. They then like to pass by the coffin for a final glimpse.

When the funeral is taking place with a Requiem Mass in church, many families like to have the dead person's body lying in church overnight before the funeral.

It is quite usual to have a Mass in church, and then for the body to be taken directly away for burial in Ireland or elsewhere. Sometimes, when the person and family have not belonged to the parish, the body goes directly to the funeral parlour. There it is quite possible to have a simple service or a Mass in the chapel of rest without going to church, before going to the airport.

To save expense, some feel they need to go directly to the cemetery or crematorium. A Mass can be said there, probably, or at least a priest can come to conduct a service.

Funeral costs

Unfortunately, funerals cost a lot. Those responsible for the arrangements have normally to expect a bill of hundreds of pounds. It can cost less to have a cremation, and of course every limousine booked for transport to church and cemetery adds heavily to the bill.

The requiem or funeral service

There is a newly published form of Funeral Rite and Mass for a Deceased Person. If no previous wishes have been recorded, it is in the hands of the next of kin or executor to work out what is wanted. This includes Mass or no Mass, music and singing as desired, the choice of readings, readers and bidding prayers.

Today the newer emphasis of the liturgy is on the Resurrection. It may seem strange to some that there should be joy coming through the sorrow, but the human and spiritual atmosphere should in fact be a mingling of tears with sure hope of the Resurrection, and therefore a certain underlying joy.

It is strange that when a person dies we can tend to say 'Poor Ann or George or whoever.' The strangeness is because we believe in the end of life and in Heaven, where each person comes into the love and peace of God. Why poor, then? On the whole I think this reflects the fact that the centre of existence for most of us is the known, the here and now earthly life. Heaven is dim and somehow far away. When life here ends, we feel the person has 'lost' their life. We do not manage to place our confidence and hope sufficiently strongly in the joy of Heaven, which we do not know from experience.

There is another consideration, which is very right and extremely important – the loss is ours. We have literally lost the presence in the body of this dearly loved relation, friend or neighbour. We shall never see them alive again in this life, hear them speak or laugh or cry, feel the warmth of their embrace and return it. As all this naturally gives us great distress, a wound and a gap in our lives. This should cause our grief to overflow in tears. Indeed it is wrong if we try to suppress this expression of emotion at our bereavement. We can do real psychological harm to ourselves by keeping a stiff upper lip. Tears are healing for all of us. We should not be shy or ashamed or think it a weakness to let go and allow our true human condition to emerge.

This rainbow combination can mean that the choice of hymns may be mixed, some of mourning and some of joy. That is a personal choice, but it is important for me to stress as well the positive, hopeful and even joyful feelings which may supervene, to the exclusion of the darker side, which can be reflected to some extent in bidding prayers and so on. In the end, the choice of tone is up to you, perhaps with the advice of the priest who will celebrate, if you think that will help.

A funeral is a most moving religious experience. It is also a personal one – families always appreciate some personalisation by the celebrant, rather than an unknown priest leading impersonally. It is one which we should share as fully as possible. It is particularly important to allow our hearts to burn within us as we listen to the Scripture, because Jesus speaks to us as he did on the road to Emmaus. And it is also important, of course, for as many as can to receive the Body and Blood of Jesus Christ in Holy Communion, which draws us so close to God and to the one who has 'gone to God'.

In the shock of Jesus dying, Lord, the women managed to remember all that needed to be done for the burial of Jesus. Help us also to be aware of the things we have to do. Give us a sense of calm and order, so that things do not get out of perspective. Let us appreciate all the help that is offered and be both warm and welcoming and also able to make the right decisions, so that everyone is satisfied, can take a part with joy, and that the atmosphere of worship and praise and hope in the resurrection pervades all our doings. Amen.

As days go by in bereavement | 9

On entering the tomb they could not find the body of the Lord Jesus. As they stood there puzzled about this, two men in brilliant clothes suddenly appeared at their side. Terrified, the women bowed their heads to the ground. But the two said to them, 'Why look among the dead for someone who is alive? He is not here. He has risen.'
(Lk.24.4–5)

Waiting and working for the funeral is a difficult period. But it is also in some ways soothing, because there are actual things which can be done, plans to be made, a sense of continuing to care for the deceased, by caring for everything that goes towards a fitting goodbye. Once the funeral service is over and the subsequent hospitality is at an end, goodbyes begin with the living. Then there may descend a silence, an emptiness, a loneliness. It really is the end of a whole period of life.

At this time, the sense of loneliness can be heightened, because it is natural that life should go on as usual – relations and friends disperse, go home, begin to take up their jobs and occupations again. While the individual or family realize this must happen, it is not so easy for them to move back into normality.

There are perhaps the initial points which should be considered and taken to heart. The truth is that bereavement cuts very deep. It cuts into the centre of a person's deeper being, bruising mind and heart alike. Ordinarily, bruising of the body takes time to come out and to lose its pain in gradual healing. Bruising of the spirit takes a far longer time, often lasting not a month but a year or more.

The second point is that despite the depth of wounding, there should and ordinarily will be a gradual lessening of pain and the beginning of a new life. This is right and is not disrespectful or un-loving towards the one who has died.

Once again, we are each individual and we react differently. This is true in bereavement as in anything else. But there is a common human strand which normally includes deep sadness, emptiness, loneliness. Ordinarily, also, there is a sense of guilt. When the last rites are behind, the past wells up in our minds and at this stage it is often not the joyful memories which predominate, but what we see as our failings. So many I have listened to in bereavement over the years bring out their sense of having failed a husband or wife, child or friend and so on. I suppose it is always true, if we look at it in one way, that we *could* have done more. But it is also true that we hold up an unreal state of perfection to ourselves and find we are wanting. Yet, the very unreality enhances our sense of deficiency and there is little or no comfort in the reassurance of a friend, counsellor or priest. The anxiety and guilt can cover any aspect of life, but it frequently has much to do with the last illness, and even failure to be at the hospital or bedside when the person died.

Anger can also erupt against doctors, nurses, the hospital staff who, in the mind, could also have done more, have perhaps saved the life; or against members of the family who were not supportive, against the priest for not visiting – and so on. All these may seen genuinely real and important. We may have to live with them, and if we do so positively, they will get into the right perspective.

The instinct of some bereaved individuals, especially those living alone perhaps, is to shut themselves away and rather shun outside aid. To them I would say, and to all the bereaved, when you can face it, it is very healing and comforting to be able to share with another person or a group – so try not to allow yourself to shut your door and brood. Tears may last, memories will become more joyful and serene, less painful.

Being alongside the bereaved

In recent times, we have become more aware of the awfulness of bereavement, its effect upon the bereaved and the possibility of coming close to them in a supportive way. In older family groupings in smaller communities there was a natural support among those living together as extended family or universally known in the village. Big cities isolate people and often split up families. This has led to more single people living alone – widows and widowers for instance. In turn, this leads to a need for being aware of the possibility of being alongside the bereaved in their distress.

a) The individual support

If we already know the bereaved as relation, friend or neighbour, we already have a way to be alongside them. We may well have known, been friendly with or loved the one who has died. This means a common grieving and a background of knowledge which needs no introduction. But sensitivity and discretion are enormously valuable, so that we are truly supportive, and neither neglect nor overwhelm the person we are trying to reach out to.

However, if we are strangers to each other, it is necessary to explain why we have come – I've come from the church, I'm from the S.V.P., and so on – or I just thought I'd drop in in case you were feeling very lonely and low, etc. The bereaved needs to know our credentials. And before we leave, it is good to promise to come again, if that seems a good idea. It can be important to a person alone in their grief to have a focal point ahead to look forward to.

There may be very practical things we can do such as promising hospitality, if they will come out, or helping with food. Some may be very lost over the rent or bills, sorting out clothes, making sure they can still stay in their rented accommodation and so on. But more than anything else, it may be the support of presence to soften the sense of abandonment, a closeness, a warmth, an embrace. Depth of sharing and relationship grow over time. They need patience and a great understanding – an ability to listen and not to say too much. From this listening we may be able to pick up different areas of loss and worry, beyond the sheer absence of physical presence and the emotional consequences. For instance one widow whose husband had been blind for all their married life had devoted the major part of her time to him, especially after the children had grown up. She read to him, drove him about, wrote letters for him and so on. After his fairly quick dying, her days were literally empty of her main occupation and delight. At this stage, she found great comfort in coming to Mass and in the support of her children – and gradually her life began to fill in new and different ways.

Of course, if we are there to be supportive, we must try to respond to demands, which can be time-consuming and which cannot necessarily (and hopefully will not) continue indefinitely but must also be utterly trustworthy with the confidences the bereaved may share with us. It is not a good thing for us to allow anyone to become dependent on us. Rather we can help them to re-establish themselves in their own right.

b) The Bereavement Group

There is an increasing growth in bereavement groups – both secular and in parishes. Some people find immediately after bereavement that they cannot face sharing their sorrow 'publicly' in a group set-up. But where groups have gathered or been gathered together, the support and joy which comes from them is both deep and tangible. And so, if possible, bereaved individuals can gradually be steered towards a group – but not hurried.

What shape the group takes will depend on the leader and also the members. The one which we have is run once a month by a religious sister. It begins with introductions and socialising, and begins or ends with a cup of tea. There is some sharing of experience in the group, a spiritual input. In the middle each person lights a candle which is struck in a bowl of sand in memory of the deceased person they are commemorating. Now and then, the session ends with a Mass in the room where the meeting takes place.

One of the outcomes of a bereavement group and indeed of individual bereavement is the opportunity to encourage the bereaved to help those more recently at loss than themselves, whether in the group or not. This is very therapeutic, and also spreads the engagement to share more widely with others a real experience of one's own.

> *Lord God, the funeral is over, everyone has gone. I feel very alone, very weary, very empty. I know that from here life goes on, but I do so much need to know that you are with me... and that he/she is with you. Give me a sense of this loving life with you of the one I love so much. And then, Lord, feeling guilty and angry and full of tears, help me to begin slowly to rise again to a new kind of living, a living separated from him/her physically, but joined closely in spirit. I know grieving will be perhaps a long and*

certainly a painful time, but I live in hope of the resurrection of myself soon in this world, and an everlasting rising with you, God of love, in your kingdom of love. Amen.

Living again after death | **10**

We believe that, if we died with Christ, then we shall live with him too. We know that Christ has been raised from the dead and will never die again. Death has no power over him any more. For by dying, he is dead to sin once and for all, and now the life that he lives is life with God. In the same way, you must see yourselves as being dead to sin but alive to God in Christ Jesus.
(Rom.6.8–11)

To lose someone we love in death – to be bereaved – is in a real sense partly to die oneself. Death is not complete for the bereaved. But depending on the closeness of the living relationship, more or less physical and sense and emotional life ceases at the death of the loved one.

However, actual life as an ordinary person goes on relentlessly. Time waits for no one! So that, when a person tries to stop the clock and to leave everything as it was in the bedroom, in the house and so on, the bereaved person dies further by failing to live in time.

If we have a basically right concept of the God of Love, we should realise that God is life and gives all things in creation life. For us he is the author and giver of life, here and in the next world. It is part of our relationship with God to live this earthly life and live it to the full. Moreover, if we accept God in our belief – and Heaven – we have to accept that the one we love is alive with God. To try to keep that person dead in this world by a closed room, a refusal to allow our thoughts of him/her to go beyond death in this life is to lose the reality of our belief, our trust and our love of God.

In Heaven all right and wrong is taken up in love. The one we love cannot hold anything against us – so away with any sense of guilt we have. God's will is our peace – to do his will here and now by loving God, our neighbour and ourselves. Surely you cannot imagine the one you love *wanting* you to be miserable and filled with gloom and only half-alive? And God does not want us to be like that either.

And so, though there will always be a gap in life, our mourning can be turned to joy, and we can rise again with Jesus in a new life which will be different, tinged with sorrow, but can be fulfilled and joyful. This does not dishonour but rather honours the memory of the deceased.

At the end of World War II there was a sergeant signaller, John. He had married just before he was posted abroad, but had no child. I was discharged and went to train for the priesthood in Rome, but he remained in Italy in the army. From there he wrote and continued to do so on his return to England. Later he wrote in great sorrow that his wife had died giving birth to their first child, but the child was all right. Later again he wrote that he wanted to marry again – a very close friend of his late wife and himself. He said both sets of parents were set against it, said it was too soon, said he only wanted a mother-substitute for the child. What did I think he should do? Knowing him very well, I trusted him completely and backed them to marry. Then he asked me to be his best man. I was proud and delighted to come from the theological college in Rome in the summer holidays in the rather unecumenical late 1940s to stand beside him at the wedding in his local Church of England parish church. In the mid-1980s when I last stayed with them at their home their two children were successful adults and John and Doris still happily fulfilled in marriage.

And this is not unique, either in the past or today. Not only in a new marriage but in so many other ways there is plenty to be done in a 'second life' – for oneself, for God and for other people. Some have even become monks, priests and nuns! Many have been the mainstay of their families, of their neighbours or of the local church.

The closing word is, therefore, that we move through death, not just into death. We move in our final death in this world to a final life in the next. But meanwhile we may have to go through a number of deaths, or bereavements, after which we can – should – must rise again to life, a new life in this world.

HE IS RISEN, ALLELUIA

Come, Lord Jesus, into this new life you have asked me to live… a life after death. Just as you once set your face resolutely towards Jerusalem, so I am setting my face, my mind and my heart to living here without the one I loved so well. But I realise, Lord, that if you will help me, I can be increased and deepened in my love of you, while I allow to grow the affection and love of those around me. They are so caring and want so much to be with me in my grief. Lord, sometimes I want to be alone with my sorrow, but I also know I must rise again, supported by so much loving kindness round about me. May I rise again to praise you and love you and serve you. Amen. Alleluia.

Appendix A.
Support Organizations

1. National, non-denominational:

   CRUSE (for widows, widowers and their children)
   126 Sheen Road, Richmond, Surrey. TW9 1VR

   THE COMPASSIONATE FRIENDS (for parents)
   6 Denmark Street, Bristol BS1 5DQ

   THE WAR WIDOWS ASSOCIATION OF GREAT BRITAIN
   17, The Earls Croft, Coventry CV3 5ES

   STILLBIRTH ASSOCIATION, Foundation for the Study of Infant Death

   GINGERBREAD (single parent families)

2. Catholic:

   The Catholic Association of Widows
   84 Baldwins Lane, Croxley Green, Rickmansworth Herts WD3 3LP

3. The Bereavement Support Service

This is a non-profit making telephone advisory service organized by one of the largest funeral directing groups in Britain, PFG Hodgson Kenyon International plc. It covers eleven subjects related to bereavement, including Making a Will, Arranging a Funeral and Coping with Bereavement. The messages, narrated by Sir Harry Secombe, are on 0898 numbers charged (May 1990) at 38p per minute peak time and 25p per minute off peak.

A free leaflet listing all the numbers may be obtained from PFG Hodgson Kenyon Bereavement Support Service, 2 Hogshead Road, Handsworth, Birmingham B21 0LT, or local branches of the group. Supplies are made available to GPs, nursing staff, clergy, solicitors etc.

Appendix B: Useful Books

All the End is a Harvest: An Anthology for those who grieve: ed. Agnes Whitaker (DLT)

Any Ward, Any Hospital: Roger Grainger (Bible Reading Fellowship)

Can I Forget You? Coping with Widowhood: Pamela Winfield (Constable)

Children, Death and Bereavement: Pat Wynne Jones (Scripture Union)

Coping with Suicide: Dr Donald Scott (Sheldon Press)

The end is the beginning. Briefing 90 (12 January 1990) (Catholic Media Office) (see extract on p.75)

A Grief Observed: C.S.Lewis (Collins)

Healing the Dying: Mary Jane, Dennis and Matthew Linn (Paulist Press)

Helping Children to Cope with Grief: Rosemary Wells (Sheldon Press)

Helplessness and Hope. Pastoral Care in Terminal Illness: Bruce D.Rumbold (SCM Press)

Letting Go: Ian Ainsworth and Peter Speck (S.P.C.K.)

Living with Dying: Cicely Saunders and Mary Barnes (Oxford University Press)

Out of the Depth: Robert Dodd (Abingdon Press)

Prayers before and after bereavement: Michael Hollings & Etta Gullick (McCrimmons)

Prayers for the Depressed: Michael Hollings & Etta Gullick (McCrimmons)

The Shade of his Hand: Michael Hollings & Etta Gullick (McCrimmons)

Sharing the Darkness: Sheila Cassidy (Darton, Longman & Todd)

Sheila: Healing through Dying: Saxon Walker (Arthur James)

Through Grief – the bereavement journey: Elizabeth Collick (DLT)

What to do after death (DHSS)

When someone you love dies: Robert Dodd (Abingdon Press)

When you are Terminally Ill: Robert Dodd (Abingdon Press)

When your Spouse dies: Cathleen L.Curry (Ave Maria Press)

Appendix C.
Do's and Dont's in Grief
S. Lieberman

Advice on how to cope with the loss of a loved on
can be given freely, but it is often very difficult to
follow advice which asks that people face pain and
suffering rather than avoid it.

The following general guidelines can be given to
any person who is bereft:

Don't avoid your feelings of anger.

Don't avoid your feelings of sadness.

Don't use drugs or alcohol in order to 'blot out'
your feelings.

Don't isolate yourself from other people.

Don't prevent other members of your family
from talking about your relative.

Don't be afraid to discuss your feelings about
your relative with friends, relatives or helpers.

Don't copy your dead relative's thoughts, ideas
or behaviour unless you really consciously want
to do so.

Don't hesitate to ask for help if you have
recurrent nightmares about your dead relative.

Don't place your dead relative on a pedestal or
idealize them.

Do notice if your feelings worsen on anniversary
dates which were important to your dead relative.

Don't rush your grief in order to get it over with
quickly.

Don't prolong your grief in order to keep the memory of your relative painfully fresh.

Don't hide away your photos or other memorabilia to avoid grief.

For those who have to cope with relative or friends who are bereft the following guidelines may be of use:

Don't overprotect your relative.

Don't insist on your relatives being 'treated' as if they were ill.

Don't be offended at your relative's angry feelings.

Don't compulsively try to 'cheer up' your relative.

Don't help your relative to avoid thinking about the object of their loss.

Don't avoid talking about the loss in order to protect your relative.

Do encourage your relative to express his/her feelings.

Appendix D.
Bereavement:
Paddy Yorkstone

(British Medical Journal 11 April 1981, 282 1224–1225)

The break-up of the extended family, a conspiracy of silence surrounding death, and a lack of mourning ritual leave many bereaved unsupported. At this vulnerable time they may turn increasingly to doctors and health workers for help.

After a death families, friends, and neighbours often offer immediate help to comfort the bereaved and deal with the practicalities of funeral arrangements. The critical period follows when this help ceases and the initial feelings of numbness or shock give way to intense grief. Although for many grieving will take its normal painful course, some (perhaps a quarter to a third) will be at risk during this time if unsupported.

Risk factors

(1) Sudden, unexpected, and untimely death – for example, fatal accident or suicide in a child or young adult.

(2) Demands of dependants: children and others.

(3) Lack of a close relationship or a warm, supportive family. Presence of a family who block attempts to grieve – for example, after stillbirth or neonatal death.

(4) Financial hardship and housing difficulties.

(5) non-employment: at home all day – particularly mothers of young children and the elderly.

(6) Earlier difficulties in accepting impending death; clinging and pining or excessive anger and self-reproach.

(7) Multiple losses.

(8) Vulnerable personality – for example, history of mental illness or inadequacy.

Problems facing the bereaved

(1) Practical difficulties in taking over unaccustomed functions of the deceased: widow, business affairs; widower, domestic responsibilities and child caring.

(2) Physical symptoms, which are normal physiological accompaniments of grief, may be self-perpetuated by the bereaved's fear for his own future health – for example, tachycardia, anorexia, insomnia, indigestion, and headache.

(3) Loneliness and isolation often increased by the community's embarrassment and inability to mention the death or the deceased.

(4) Dealing with the grief of other members of the family in addition to his or her own: particularly hard for the surviving parent of young children.

(5) The frightening intensity of grief, sometimes accompanied by feelings of panic or suicidal thoughts (no diffidence should be felt in asking a direct question about suicide).

(6) Fears of 'breakdown' often spoken of after experiencing vivid illusions: 'sights' or 'sounds' of the dead person, or forgetfulness.

(7) Lack of an outlet for the expression of guilt and anger.

Needs of the bereaved

(1) To be allowed to talk about the experience: the illness, death, funeral, and memories.

(2) To have expressions of grief accepted.

(3) To know that some guilt and anger is usual and to be able to talk of this although it may be directed towards the care givers.

(4) Sometimes the bereaved need protection from well meaning 'escape' routes urged upon them too soon or from attempts to stop them grieving – for example, change of house or job; prolonged visits to friends or family to delay returning to the empty house.

(5) Direction towards sources of practical help: Citizens Advice Bureau; Department of Health and Social Security booklet *What do do after a Death*.

(6) The first anniversary is a crucial event; a contact around this period is greatly appreciated and it is a good time to assess the progress of the bereaved person.

(7) The need of children to grieve is not always recognised and shared in families and some will require special help.

(8) Occasionally the bereaved need 'permission' to stop grieving and require help to adapt to new roles.

(9) A lifeline: a phone number or other means of contact. Many bereaved are vulnerable and insecure and often unable to make demands or ask for help. An appointment not kept or promise of contact not fulfilled can be devastating.

Appendix E.
Extracts from 'Briefing', Vol. 20 no 1, 12 Jan 1990

The care of the terminally ill

The most important thing to remember about those who are facing death is that they are people on a journey into the unknown and that they are often terribly afraid. They suffer too the agony of loss and alienation as their failing health separates them daily still further from strength, physical beauty, ability to work, role as bread-winner or mistress of the house and all the other human activities and attributes which we all take for granted.

It frequently happens, too, that this fear and loss are compounded by a terrible loneliness because those closest to them simply don't know what to say or do and therefore either distance themselves or behave in such a way that, quite unintentionally, causes terrible pain. How then can ordinary people best help those who are dying, or those who are losing or have lost someone they love? Perhaps there are two basic things to remember: by yourself – because the sick or bereaved remain themselves – even if they are physically altered by illness or grief. The great temptation we all have is to divide the world into 'us' and 'them' categories because we find that safer.

The 'us' in our lives are our family and friends and the other 'ordinary' people; the 'them' are the dropouts, those in prison, the HIV positive – the insane, the immoral – and the dying. But the dying are really 'us' fallen on hard times – (just like the rest of 'them'!) and we must resist the tendency to distance ourselves. We must stay alongside, talking as we always used to, loving, laughing, hugging, sharing, telling jokes, and so on, And if our friends want to talk about their pain, their fear or their loss we should stay our ground and listen.

The other great mistake people make about accompanying the dying is that they feel they must be able to say something wise and helpful, and they shy away because they feel at a loss for words. The real truth, however, is that what most of us need when we're in trouble is someone to listen to us and respond with warmth and understanding. The dying know that their family and friends are sad and at a loss and they don't expect any world-shattering wisdom – but they long for someone to share their pain and bewilderment, their anger and their fear. What they want is not our pity – being sorry for them, but our 'empathy' – our being sorry with them... Training in effective listening and counsell-ing is very important for those who wish to work professionally with the dying and the bereaved. For most of us, however, it's a question of having the courage to walk towards the grieving rather than crossing the road to avoid confronting them. And if we do, we'll discover that, inseparable from the pain of death, there is often a rare joy and laughter; the urgency of living a shortened life drives out small talk and pretence and, once stripped of their protective facade, people are revealed with all their amazing strength, courage, beauty and generosity, as well as in their vulnerability and their foolishness. And of course, because the dying are 'us' not 'them' we too find in our empty handedness a richness of love and strength that we never knew was possible. Love is like a basket of loaves and fishes – you never have enough until you start to give it away. (pp12–13)

Strategies for unexpected dying

a. Young man, 33 years, married, 3 children, accountant, 'stress headaches' for 4 weeks, getting worse. Sent to specialist for reassurance. Scan – inoperable brain tumour, likely prognosis 3–12 weeks.

b. 11–year-old boy, Steven, pain in hip 'growing pains'. Short of breath out playing. Seen by doctor: x-rays show bone cancer in hip with 2% spread to lungs. Likely prognosis 3–12 weeks.

Because we live in a society which denies death, telling the truth about death and dying is a problem both for the medical profession and for people with serious illnesses and their families.

Old attitude was 'paternalistic'
a. Doctor sees wife alone and says this is inoperable brain tumour. 'I think we'd better not tell him. Just take home and we'll see him in the clinic in 6 weeks'.
- how can this wife relate to her husband if she has to lie to him?
- how can this man prepare for his family's future

if he doesn't know he is dying?

- How can the children be prepared if their daddy doesn't know the truth?

- how frightened will he be if he starts to lose his speech, power in his arm, has fits etc?

By age 10 children have formed ideas about death and life after death (whatever their families believe!)

  b. Steven visits outpatients department with Mum and Dad

'Hi, Steve, nice to see you and Mum and Dad again. How's the pain in your hip these days?'

'It doesn't hurt as long as I take the tablets. When can I stop taking them, Dr Alan?'

'I think you'll probably always have to take tablets or medicine for that pain, Steve. Will that be a problem?'

'Only when I go back to school, because I'll have to give them to the nurse and she might forget. When can I go back to school? Dad says I might not go back this year'.

'What makes Dad think that ?'

'Well, because he says I've got an illness that makes my hip hurt and makes me get out of breath and it's a sort of illness that can't get better, so I can't go on my skateboard anymore'.

'What do you think about that?'

'If I can't get better, then... do you think I might die like Grampa did? I asked Mum but she just got upset. I don't know if she was upset about Gramp or about me... But I think it was about me. Look, she's upset again now. Mum, I'm sorry. I'm sorry I'm sick. Please don't cry. I'm sorry'.

'Mum know it isn't your fault, Steve. Why do you think she is upset?'

'Well, if I die she'll be lonely because the little ones are too little to talk to about things. And she'll have to give my skateboard to Andy Scott, because he'd look after it. And he'll remember all the laughs we had when we were playing on it – he's my best friend, and I've promised him he can have it when I die'.

'That is very kind of you. What did he say?'

'He said his gramps died, too, so maybe I could introduce him to my grampa. I'll probably teach them both how to skateboard. Anyway, Mum and Dad are taking me for an ice cream after we've finished visiting you today'.

- by asking non-threatening questions, the doctor has learned that Steven is asking questions from his parents, receiving answers which help him to reach a new understanding of his position. He has understood he is going to die. He has understood that his mother's sadness is about separation. And he doesn't expect death to be the end of him!   (p13–15)

Bereavement counselling: Three Principles

Three principles to consider when offering support in any situation but particularly in bereavement are: i) to see people as individuals, ii) to respect their right to make decisions, and iii) to treat in confidence the things which we hear.

i) **People as individuals**. It is important to recognise each person as an individual and to allow them to emerge unpressurised by other people's experiences and expectations. To draw too many parallels with the experience of other widow/widowers/bereaved parents etc., denies the bereaved person the opportunity to be seen as and for themselves. Neither should our own style of coping with situations or cultural expectations stand in the way of our trying to see clearly what is happening to a particular bereaved person.

ii) **Making decisions**. It can be tempting when people are in need to assume that their vulnerability makes it difficult for them to make decisions. This can be particularly true when dealing with the elderly. Further distress will arise if people are deprived of making choices for themselves on issues of personal importance. Unless care is taken it can be another way in which the by-product of loss is more loss, with a consequent reduction in self-esteem for the bereaved.

iii) **Confidentiality**. If we offer appropriate listening to the bereaved, many personal feelings and much private information will be shared. It is essential, even if this occurs during an informal visit, that information is treated confidentially. Special reassurance needs to be conveyed to the bereaved person that we can be trusted not to share the things we have heard. (p.19)